W9-BEG-119

STARS OF NASCAR

Dale Earnhardt Jr.

BY MATT DOEDEN

Reading Consultant:
Barbara J. Fox
Reading Specialist
North Carolina State University

Content Consultant:
Betty L. Carlan
Research Librarian
International Motorsports Hall of Fame
Talladega, Alabama

Mankato, Minnesota

Blazers is published by Capstone Press,
151 Good Counsel Drive, P.O. Box 669, Mankato, Minnesota 56002.
www.capstonepress.com

Printed in the United States of America

Library of Congress Cataloging-in-Publication Data
Doeden, Matt.
Dale Earnhardt Jr. / by Matt Doeden.
p. cm. — (Blazers. Stars of NASCAR)
Summary: "Explores the life and racing career of NASCAR Sprint Cup star Dale Earnhardt Jr." — Provided by publisher.
Includes bibliographical references and index.
ISBN-13: 978-1-4296-1975-2 (hardcover)
ISBN-10: 1-4296-1975-9 (hardcover)
1. Earnhardt, Dale, Jr. — Juvenile literature. 2. Automobile racing drivers — United States — Biography — Juvenile literature. I. Title. II. Series

GV1032.E19D65 2009
796.72092 — dc22
[B] 2007052187

Essential content terms are **bold** and are defined on the spread where they first appear.

Editorial Credits
Abby Czeskleba, editor; Bobbi J. Wyss, designer; Jo Miller, photo researcher

Photo Credits
AP Images/Paul Kizzie, 20–21; Rusty Burroughs, 29; Terry Renna, 6–7
Corbis/GT Images/George Tiedemann, cover (Earnhardt)
Getty Images for NASCAR/Rusty Jarrett, 24–25
Getty Images Inc./Chris Graythen, cover (car); David Taylor, 14–15, 16–17; Jamie Squire, 8–9; Jonathan Ferrey, 4–5; Layne Murdoch, 26–27; RacingOne, 10–11, 12–13, 18–19
The Sharpe Image/Sam Sharpe, 22–23
Shutterstock/Anastasios Kandris (speed and racing icons, throughout); Bocos Benedict (abstract digital background, throughout); Rzymu (flag background, throughout)

1 2 3 4 5 6 13 12 11 10 09 08

TABLE OF CONTENTS

Dale Earnhardt Jr. trailing Tony Stewart

DAYTONA CHAMPION

Dale Earnhardt Jr. was in second place at the 2004 Daytona 500. With just 20 laps left, his red and white number 8 car sped around the track.

Dale Jr. was chasing Tony Stewart's orange number 20 car. Dale Jr. faked a pass **high**. Stewart moved up to block him. But Dale Jr. ducked **low** before Stewart could move. Dale Jr. sailed by for the lead!

high — the outside part of the track
low — the inside part of the track

Bud
CHAMPION
CINCINNATI
SERIES

Stewart tried to retake the lead. But Dale Jr. fought him off. The fans roared as the number 8 car took the **checkered flag**. Dale Jr. had won the race!

checkered flag — a flag with a pattern of black and white squares, used to signal when the first car has crossed the finish line

BORN TO RACE

Dale Earnhardt Jr. was born October 10, 1974, in Concord, North Carolina. He bought his own car when he was 17 years old. He raced it at a local track.

Dale Jr. (left) racing in his Legend Series car

TRACK FACT!

Dale Jr. paid $200 for his first race car.

Dale Jr. (far left) with his stepmom and dad in 1986

Dale Jr. watched his dad, Dale Earnhardt Sr., win NASCAR races and championships. Dale Jr. dreamed of racing in NASCAR himself.

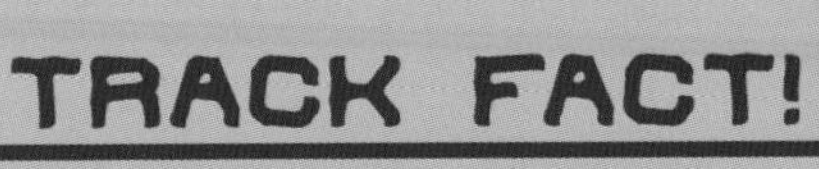
TRACK FACT!

Dale Earnhardt Sr. won seven NASCAR Cup championships. He and Richard Petty share the record for most Cup championships won.

Dale Jr. raced on small tracks for several years. In 1997, he joined his dad's NASCAR team, Dale Earnhardt Incorporated (DEI).

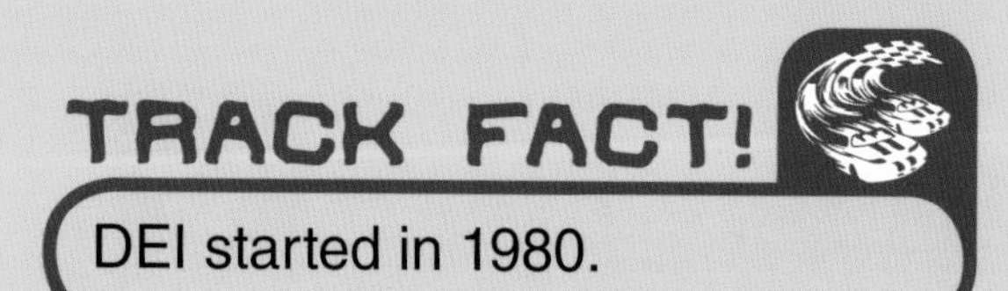

31
Wrangler
JEANS
R/R 1-800-888-BUCK
BUSCH
BUSCH
CLEVITE
MCI
JESEL
Holley
MOOG
MOROSO
SIMPSON
PENSKE

ACDelco
BUSCH SERIES
CHAMPIONS
NASCAR
BUSCH
SERIES
GRAND NATIONAL DIVISION
RAPIDFIRE
BURGER KING
NABISCO
Coca-Cola
Snap-on
ACDelco

Dale Jr. struggled in his first year in the **Busch Series**. But in 1998, he won his first race. He went on to win the Busch Series championship that year. He won it again in 1999.

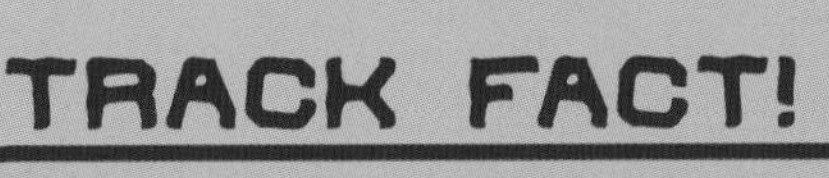

TRACK FACT!

Dale Jr. is the only third-generation NASCAR champion. His grandpa, Ralph Earnhardt, and his dad were named two of NASCAR's "50 Greatest Drivers" in 1998.

Busch Series – NASCAR's second-highest level of competition where drivers gain experience before moving on to the Cup Series

CUP SERIES STAR

In 2000, Dale Jr. was ready to move full-time to the ***Cup Series***. He drove the number 8 car for DEI. He won his first Cup race at Texas Motor Speedway on April 2, 2000.

Cup Series — NASCAR's highest level of competition

Dale Jr. after winning the 2000 Pontiac Excitement 400

Dale Sr. (left) and Dale Jr. (right)

The 2001 season started with a tragedy. Dale Sr. was killed in a crash on February 18, 2001, at the Daytona 500. It was one of the hardest times in Dale Jr.'s life.

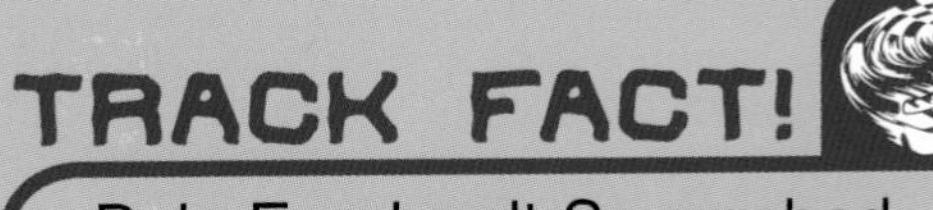

Dale Earnhardt Sr. crashed during the last lap of the 2001 Daytona 500.

Dale Jr. and his DEI teammates kept racing. He knew that was what his dad would have wanted. In 2003, Dale Jr. finished third in the Cup standings.

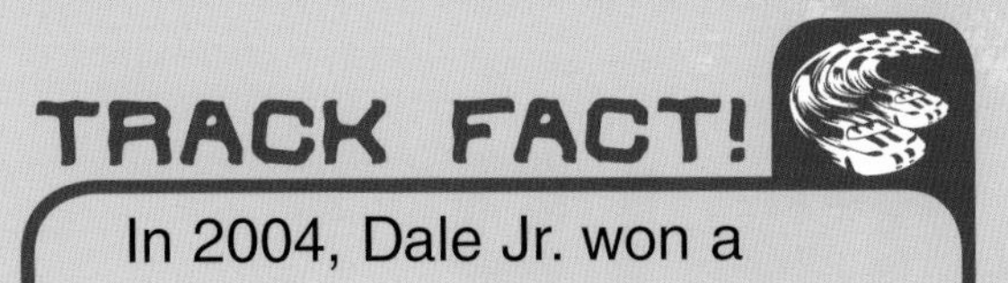

TRACK FACT!

In 2004, Dale Jr. won a career-best six Cup races.

DALE JR. TODAY

Recent years have been tough for Dale Jr. In 2005, he finished in 19th place. He did not make the **Chase for the Cup**. He took fifth place in 2006 but won only one race. In 2007, he finished in 16th place.

Chase for the Cup — the last 10 races of the Cup season in which the top 12 drivers battle for the championship

TRACK FACT!

In 2007, the number of drivers in the Chase for the Cup changed from 10 to 12.

Dale Jr. needed a change. He left DEI at the end of the 2007 season. In 2008, he started driving the number 88 car for Hendrick Motorsports. With Hendrick, he hopes to finally win his first Cup championship.

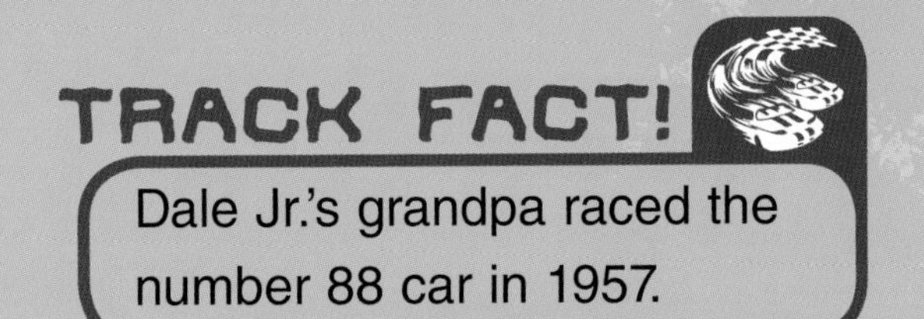

TRACK FACT!

Dale Jr.'s grandpa raced the number 88 car in 1957.

CUP CAREER STATISTICS

Dale Earnhardt Jr.'s Cup Statistics

Year	Races	Wins	Poles	Top-5	Top-10	Winnings
1999	5	0	0	0	1	$162,095
2000	34	2	2	3	5	$2,585,475
2001	36	3	2	9	15	$5,384,627
2002	36	2	2	11	16	$4,570,976
2003	36	2	0	13	21	$4,923,497
2004	36	6	0	16	21	$7,201,380
2005	36	1	0	7	13	$5,761,832
2006	36	1	0	10	17	$5,466,104
2007	36	0	1	7	12	$5,221,975
Career	**291**	**17**	**7**	**76**	**121**	**$41,277,961**

ACDelco
ACDelco

GLOSSARY

Busch Series (BUSH SEER-eez) — NASCAR's second-highest level of competition where drivers gain experience before moving on to the Cup Series; in 2008, the series became the Nationwide Series.

Chase for the Cup — the last 10 races of NASCAR's season in which the top 12 drivers battle for the championship

checkered flag (CHEK-urd FLAG) — the flag waved at the end of a race's final lap; the winner "takes" the checkered flag.

Cup Series — NASCAR's highest level of competition; the series has been known as the Winston Cup and the Nextel Cup; it is now called the Sprint Cup.

high — the outside part of the track

low — the inside part of the track

pole — the inside spot in the front row of cars at the start of a race; drivers earn the pole by having the best qualifying time.

tragedy (TRAJ-uh-dee) — a very sad event

READ MORE

Armentrout, David, and Patricia Armentrout. *Dale Earnhardt Jr.* Discover the Life of a Sports Star II. Vero Beach, Fla.: Rourke, 2005.

Eagen, Rachel. *NASCAR.* Automania! New York: Crabtree, 2007.

Savage, Jeff. *Dale Earnhardt Jr.* Amazing Athletes. Minneapolis: Lerner, 2006.

INTERNET SITES

FactHound offers a safe, fun way to find Internet sites related to this book. All of the sites on FactHound have been researched by our staff.

WWW.FACTHOUND.COM®

Here's how:

1. Visit *www.facthound.com*
2. Choose your grade level.
3. Type in this book ID **1429619759** for age-appropriate sites. You may also browse subjects by clicking on letters, or by clicking on pictures and words.
4. Click on the **Fetch It** button.

FactHound will fetch the best sites for you!

INDEX